The Extraordinary R~~~~ of Orca ~

of

TRISTRAM

Henry

Alice

A Note To The Director...

This is a one-act version of a play entitled **The Secret Lives Of Henry & Alice.** Like the full-length original, it's a virtuouso piece for two talented and versatile performers - one male, one female. There is a suggestion in the text that the couple are around forty years old, but the play works perfectly well with actors aged anywhere between thirty and fifty.

As Henry & Alice act out their fantasies, they are required to become a number of different characters, sometimes reverting quite suddenly back to their original personae. In order to help the actors clarify their roles, the script gives the name of the relevant fantasy character who is speaking at every point.

The set requirements may be treated as literally or figuratively as you wish, and for that reason no official properties list is given.

Clearly, however, the play is best served by the creative use of a few simple and symbolic props (supplemented with some mime for the fantasy sequences) together with atmospheric lighting - particularly spotlights - to convey the fast switches of scene.

A Flying Ducks Publication

Rights of Performance by Amateurs and Professionals are controlled by **Samuel French Limited, 52, Fitzroy Street, London, W1P 6JR.** Samuel French, or their authorized agents, issue licences on payment of a fee.

It is an infringement of the Copyright to give any performance or public reading of this play before the fee has been paid and the licence issued.

The publication of this play does not imply that it is necessarily available for performance by amateurs or professionals, either in the British Isles or Overseas.

Amateurs and Professionals considering a production are strongly advised, in their own interests, to apply to Samuel French, or their overseas agents, for consent before starting rehearsals or booking a theatre or hall.

VIDEO RECORDING OF AMATEUR PRODUCTIONS

Please note that the copyright laws governing video-recording are extremely complex and that it should not be assumed that any play may be video recorded for whatever purpose without first obtaining the permission of the appropriate agents. The fact that a play is published does not indicate that video rights are available or that Samuel French Ltd control such rights.

For more information on Flying Ducks Publications, write to *Flying Ducks Publications, Station Road, Highley, Shropshire* WV16 6NW.

ISBN 1 900997 00 2

THE EXTRAORDINARY REVELATIONS
OF
ORCA THE GOLDFISH

A spotlight picks up Henry, sitting centre-stage on a settee. He addresses the audience directly.

Henry Hello, I'm Henry Olivier, and welcome to *An Evening With Henry Olivier*. Where to begin? I suppose the first question most people ask me is "Are you related to the great Laurence Olivier?" Well, surprisingly enough, no, I'm not. I first met Larry back in the sixties - he was doing his Lear, I was doing my Hamlet - and he'd got a night off and came to see my performance.

Alice has entered in the background, passing momentarily through the spotlight, tidying up the room. Her interjections are at first ignored by Henry.

Alice Henry...
Henry After that, of course, Larry and I became great friends...
Alice Have you made the tea, Henry?
Henry ...and we'd go and see each other's shows whenever we could...
Alice Henry, have you made the tea?
Henry ...though, of course, it wasn't always possible, what with the heavy schedules...
Alice Henry...
Henry ...because, well, in our own ways, Larry and I were both workaholics...
Alice (*screaming*) Henry!!!

The full stage lights come on with a jolt. Henry is shocked out of his daydream.

Henry (*bad-tempered*) What??
Alice Oh, honestly. Sometimes you're in a world of your own.
Henry I was listening.
Alice I asked you half an hour ago to make the tea, and have you done it?
Henry I'm doing it now, Alice.
Alice Why didn't you do it half an hour ago, Henry?
Henry If I'd made the tea half an hour ago, Alice, it would now be cold. I thought you'd prefer a fresh cup.

A Flying Ducks Publication

Alice Perhaps you think I should make the tea, Henry?
Henry Not if you're busy, Alice.
Alice I'm tidying up, Henry.

The lights close on Henry, who turns to address the audience again. The convention of addressing the audience directly signifies a daydream, during which the other character cannot hear, and therefore does not react to, any words spoken. Henry is also invisible to Alice, and struts around her as he speaks.

Henry Oh, where are my manners? Let me introduce you to my wife, Alice. She's tidying up at the moment. That's what Alice does. She tidies up. I make a mess, she tidies up. Quite a good arrangement really. We keep each other in work. She loves it. Ironing. Washing dishes. Hoovering. Wiping off the worksurfaces. I worked it out once. She spends three and a half weeks a year just wiping off worksurfaces. I try to do my bit, you know. Modern man, and all that. A few Christmases ago I even made the ultimate male sacrifice - I bought her a dishwasher. I mean, any other woman would have been thrilled to bits, but not my Alice. Do you know what she said?

The lighting again changes mood, and Alice now takes up the action in a flashback. She's holding a tiny scrap of paper, wrapped in Christmas paper.

Alice What's this?
Henry Open it! I was going to pop it in a really big box or something, just to disguise it, as a surprise, sort of thing. But in the end I didn't think it was worth bothering.

She's now unwrapped the present, and is staring blankly at the little scrap of paper.

Alice What is it?
Henry What does it look like?
Alice I don't know.
Henry It's a dishwasher!
Alice It doesn't look like a dishwasher.
Henry Well, it's not exactly a dishwasher, it's the receipt deposit thing the man gave me. I've put fifty quid down on it. They're delivering it next week.
Alice (*totally bemused*) You've bought us a dishwasher?
Henry No, I've bought you a dishwasher. You're the one that does the dishes, nine times out of ten.

A Flying Ducks Publication

Alice Ten times out of ten.

Henry Even better. Well?

Alice Well what?

Henry Do you like it?

Alice I don't know.

Henry Don't know? What do you mean, you don't know?

Alice Well, I need to know a bit more about it.

Henry What do you mean, a bit more about it? What do you need to know about a dishwasher?

Alice Well, what sort is it?

Henry What do you mean, what sort is it?

Alice What sort is it?

Henry (*getting increasingly angry*) The dishwashing sort. The sort that washes dishes. What does it matter what sort?

Alice Well, how big is it?

Henry Big enough to wash dishes.

Alice Well what make is it?

Henry What is this? Twenty questions?

Alice You bought it, Henry, you must at least know what make it is!

Henry It's a good make! It's a bloody...Sony or something, what the hell does it matter?

Alice Well, just tell me something about it, Henry, at least - I mean, what colour is it?

Henry Fucking orange!

Alice Henry!

Henry What colour do you think it is, Alice? It's a dishwasher! It's white!

Alice There's no need to get angry!

Henry I had a choice of white ones and white ones, so I played safe, Alice. I chose a sodding white one.

Alice And you can't remember anything else about it.

Henry I can remember it cost me two hundred and fifty quid. I can remember thinking that my wife is going to be thrilled to bits on Christmas day. I can remember thinking that this is the best idea for a present I've ever had.

Alice It's not very personal.

Henry Course it's bloody personal. How much more personal can you get? You're the one that does the bloody washing up, aren't you?

Alice Stop swearing.

Henry So who's going to benefit from it, Alice? Eh? You. Not me. I'm not going to get any pleasure out of it. When all the dinner plates are piled up in a big heap on Sunday afternoon, who's going to be able to sit back for the first time in her life and put her feet up, eh? Not me. You!

Alice So, you'll scrape all the plates and load up the dishwasher for me, will you, Henry?

Henry Oh, come on, Alice, now you're getting lazy.

The lights instantly cut to a spotlight on Henry, who turns to the audience.

Henry But she couldn't see it. I took the receipt back in the end. Had my money back. It only dawned on me later that the reason Alice didn't want a dishwasher is that she actually likes doing the washing up. She'd be lost without it. (*The lights fade half back up, to reveal Alice searching around the settee*) She's looking for the other slipper at the moment. I've left it behind the settee tonight, just to spice up the evening. Cold. Colder. Getting warmer. Yes! Quick shake of the head. (*Alice shakes her head*) I do it on purpose. She actually enjoys hunting for slippers.

Alice He must think I actually enjoy hunting for slippers.

Henry There they go. Back by the side of the settee. Everything in its proper place.

Alice Henry!

Henry Including me.

Alice What a pig-sty.

Henry (*addressing Alice, as the full lights come back up*) I've just put the kettle on. I thought you might like a cup of tea.

Alice It was looking fine until you came home.

Henry Yes, my mistake, dear.

Alice I realize it's my job - tidying up - my little place in life.

Henry I didn't say that.

Alice You think it, Henry.

Henry No, Alice, you think I think it.

Alice I *know* you think it, Henry.

Henry You *think* you know it, Alice.

Alice All I ask is just a little helping hand here and there.

Henry Such as making the tea.

Alice Such as making the tea.

Henry I'll make the tea then, shall I?

Alice And try not to spill it all over the place again. I've only just finished wiping off the worksurfaces.

Henry I rest my case.

A Flying Ducks Publication

Henry exits. Alice stops work, and sighs, as a spotlight closes on her.

Alice Alice Smith. Housewife. Born - September 27th, 1957. Died - about fifteen years ago. Married, no children, to Henry Smith. Maiden name, Smith. Married name, Smith. That's progress. "Lovely chap, your Henry", they all say. "Wouldn't hurt a fly". Depends if you count boring one to death. Why couldn't I have married an exciting Henry? Catherine Turnbull married an exciting Henry. Henry Olivier. An actor. Done Shakespeare and everything. Been on the telly. Played the Postman in Brookside. That's her Henry. Not my Henry. Why couldn't I have married an actor?

Enter Henry, holding a melon. Lights back up.

Henry "Alas, poor Yorick. I knew him well". He never said that, apparently.
Alice Who never said what?
Henry Hamlet. He never said "I knew him well".
Alice If this is another one of your interesting facts, Henry, I'm not interested.
Henry Like Bogart. He never said "Play it again, Sam".
Alice Did he ever say "Make the tea"?
Henry It's done.
Alice About time.
Henry Can't hurry a boiling kettle, Alice. Basic physics. The water has to reach a hundred degrees celsius before you can apply it to the bag. Would you like a cup, by the way?
Alice What are you doing with that melon?
Henry It's going rotten. Do you want me to throw it away?
Alice May as well. (*Henry wanders off. A spotlight closes again on Alice*) Throw our marriage away while you're at it. (*She reflects*) Did I say that? Did I mean that?

The spotlight cross-fades to one on Henry, who's about to put the melon in the bin, but stops and stares at it. He picks up a banana and brings it to his mouth, using it like a sports commentator's microphone. He adopts a heavily affected American accent, imitating the double-act of Jim and Clive - two American football commentators.

Jim I have to tell you, Clive, that all eyes in the stadium tonight will be glued on this guy - Henry Smith - the new quarterback for the Brownsocks. He may be new to the team, but this guy is no rookie.

A Flying Ducks Publication

Clive That's right, Jim, this man has an incredible record. Just one week into the job and he has already deestroyed the deefènce of the San Francisco 49'ers, and the Deetroit Spinners. Ninety-four touchdowns - a yards gainage equivalent to around six and half miles.

Jim That's right, Clive, and I gotta tell you that those cute little cheerleaders go absolutely bananas whenever this guy touches the football. Here we go again - it's first and ten on the 49'ers forty-eight, with just forty-seven seconds left to go in the forty-sixth Superbowl. Just watch those linebackers' knees tremble. Htt! Htt! Htt!

Lights cut to show Alice, on the phone.

Alice I have to say, Catherine, I'm getting very worried about him. Last night he ran screaming through the kitchen and threw a melon out of the window. If he carries on like this he'll start to get interesting. (*Henry enters*) Anyway, got to go. Speak to you later. Bye.

Henry Who was that?

Alice Catherine.

Henry Who's Catherine?

Alice My sister, Catherine.

Henry Oh. What did she want?

Alice Nothing. I rang her.

Henry Oh. What did you want?

Alice Nothing.

Henry Oh, good. Glad I got those BT shares.

Alice It was just a chat, Henry. I am allowed to say hello to my sister just once in a blue moon.

Henry Twice.

Alice What?

Henry Twice in a blue moon. You rang her yesterday.

Alice Well, I'm very sorry!

Henry Just saying.

Alice Anyway, I didn't. She rang me yesterday.

Henry What did she want?

Alice Nothing much.

Henry Oh. Pity she couldn't have tagged yesterday's nothing much onto the end of today's nothing - would have saved her phone bill.

Alice Haven't you got anything to do?

Henry Like what?

A Flying Ducks Publication

Alice Go and feed the goldfish or something.
Henry Done it.
Alice Do it again.
Henry You're not supposed to overfeed goldfish. It confuses them.
Alice Oh, go on, Henry. Live a little. Confuse the goldfish.

Henry gets up and feeds the goldfish, who is in a small, round bowl.

Henry Orca. Come on, Orca. Special treat. Come and have some more powdered plankton. It's your favourite, smoky bacon. Same as last week. And the week before. Mmm, yummy. (*Staring intensely into the bowl*) Poor sod. What a life, eh? Going round and round and round in little circles all day, every day, until you die.
Alice (*thoughtfully, with a deep sigh*) Yes.
Henry What's for tea?
Alice Fish.
Henry Right.
Alice Or you can have spaghetti.
Henry I don't mind.
Alice Well, choose one.
Henry Just surprise me.
Alice Which one do you want me to surprise you with?
Henry The one I'm not expecting.
Alice Which one are you expecting?
Henry I don't mind!
Alice Just make a choice! You've got to want one *slightly* more than the other!
Henry Why have I?
Alice You just have. Everybody does.
Henry Well, which one do you want *slightly* more than the other?
Alice I don't care - it's your choice.
Henry Why is it my choice?
Alice Because I'm not very hungry.
Henry Well I'm starving.
Alice Then choose one!
Henry Which is the quickest?
Alice The fish.
Henry We'll have the fish, then.
Alice But I want to use the spaghetti up.
Henry Well, we'll have the spaghetti then!

A Flying Ducks Publication

Alice It doesn't matter, I can use the spaghetti up tomorrow.

Henry We'll have the fish then.

Alice Look, whichever one you have today you'll have to have the other one tomorrow.

Henry Well it doesn't matter then, does it? I'll have the other one tomorrow and this one today.

Alice Which one?

Henry Whichever one you want.

Alice Well bloody choose one!

Henry No! I bloody won't!

Alice Why not?

Henry It's getting to be a matter of principle now, I don't want to bloody well choose one. I refuse to choose.

Alice Right! We'll have neither then!

Henry No, we'll have both! We'll have fish and spaghetti.

Alice Don't be ridiculous.

Henry With a glass of red and white wine.

Alice sits rigidly.

Henry What are you doing?

Alice Waiting for you to make your mind up.

A spotlight narrows on Henry. He stares intensely forward. There's the sound of distant, atmospheric military music. Alice, speaking in darkness, becomes an American Senator, Henry is the President.

Senator It's an extremely grave situation, Mr President. Failure to act now could lead to the de-stabilisation of the entire Western alliance. On the other hand, if we do act, the consequences...

President I'm quite well aware of the consequences, Senator.

Senator Yes, Mr President.

President General Montgomery?

Senator He says yes, sir. A most definite yes.

President General Thorpe?

Senator Resolutely against, sir.

President The senate?

Senator Split right down the middle. It has to be your decision, Mr President.

President How long have I got?

Senator We calculate a safe window of around fifteen seconds, sir.

A sound effect of a ticking clock builds to a climax and stops.

Senator Mr President?
President All right. Let's do it.

Full stage lights instantly fade up to signal the end of the daydream.

Alice Let's do what?
Henry Let's have the fish.
Alice Hooray.

She gets up and heads for the door.

Henry Or the spaghetti. I really don't mind.

Alice exits, disgusted. Lights to black. Pause. From the darkness we hear:

Henry What's this?
Alice What do you mean, "What's this?" It's your tea.
Henry Oh.
Alice What's wrong with it?
Henry Nothing's wrong with it. (*Pause*) I just fancied the spaghetti, that's all.

We hear the crash of a plate. Lights up to reveal Henry watching TV. Enter Alice.

Henry (*flicking through channels aimlessly with the TV remote*) Thought the snooker might be on by now.
Alice I've been thinking.
Henry Steady on, Alice.
Alice Let's have someone round to dinner.
Henry Fish, or spaghetti?
Alice I'm serious, Henry. We never *do* anything. Look at me! I'm forty-seven years old. I could just drop dead tomorrow. Then what?
Henry I'd cancel the dinner party.
Alice You never know what's round the corner, Henry. Especially at our age. I mean, look at Derek Simmons from down the road. Only fifty-one. He's just had his leg amputated for the third time.

Henry (*pause for thought*) He's done what?
Alice Well, you know what I mean.
Henry What is he - a bloody centipede?
Alice They had to keep taking bits off. Higher and higher. Creeping whatsit.
Henry Creeping whatsit?
Alice Blood clots or something - I don't know. Caused some sort of blockage in his main archery. *He'll* never play tennis again.
Henry Archery?
Alice You have to get the most out of life, Henry, while you can.
Henry I don't like tennis. Or archery.
Alice We never go out. Normal couples go out.
Henry Who's normal?
Alice Jim took Anthea to his works do the other night. They had a great time. They all had to dress up in leather.
Henry Where does he work - a sex shop?
Alice No! They had one of those Biafran nights.
Henry A what?
Alice You know, with the accordion player and the oompah band.
Henry Bavarian night, you daft old sod!
Alice That's what I meant.
Henry Bloody Biafran night.
Alice Oh, shut up.
Henry I bet the food wasn't up to much.
Alice Oh, grow up!

Alice storms out. A spotlight narrows on Henry, as he stands. His eyes blur into a daydream. There's a gentle sound effect of a party, and the latter-day Noel Coward starts acknowledging a series of imaginary guests.

Henry "Hi!" "Hello there." "Hi, thanks for coming."

Enter Samantha.

Sam Hi.
Henry Hello.
Sam You must be Henry.
Henry That's right.
Sam I'm Samantha.
Henry Hello, Samantha.

A Flying Ducks Publication

Sam My closest friends call me Sam.
Henry In that case, hello Sam.
Sam Great party.
Henry Thanks. More champers?
Sam I shouldn't, it goes right to my head. A few sips and I start losing control of my body.
Henry Pint or half?
Sam What the hell. You're only young and incredibly sensuous once.
Henry Where's your husband this evening?
Sam Work's party. They're having a Bavarian night.
Henry Oh? Where?
Sam In Bavaria.
Henry I see.
Sam Look, Henry, at the risk of sounding a little forward, I do find you outrageously attractive, and when all the other guests have left, I'd very much like you to pluck me up in your strong arms, tear the clothes from my thrashing limbs, toss me like a rag doll onto the sofa, and roger me senseless.
Henry I see.
Sam If that's all right.
Henry Look, Sam, maybe I'm an old-fashioned kind of guy, but when a lady asks me to roger her senseless, I usually take it as a bit of a come-on.
Sam Do we have a date?
Henry We have a date.
Sam Oh, one last thing. Is it all right if I pour whipped cream over your lower torso and then slowly lick my way up your inner thighs?
Henry Let me think about it. (*A five second pensive pause*) Okay.
Sam Good. I'm going to mingle. Great party.
Henry Thanks for coming.
Sam Let's not count our chickens.
Henry Sam.
Sam Mmm?
Henry Can I kiss you?
Sam No. But you can gently squeeze one of my breasts.

Henry leans forward tentatively, and is just on the verge of touching her breast when the daydream is broken.

Alice What the hell are you doing!
Henry I erm...bit of fluff on your dress.

A Flying Ducks Publication

Alice I'm going to have a bath.

Alice struts off, bewildered.

Henry Bloody Biafran night. Friends round to dinner. Course, I know what all this is leading up to. Seen it all before. A few days of the old "What's life all about?" routine, just to soften me up, then out come the exotic holiday brochures. You know the sort of thing. African safari. Far East experience. Once in a lifetime cruise. She'll be intoxicated by the romantic setting. And I'll utter those three little words. No bloody chance.

A sunny spotlight hits Alice, now blissfully reclined in a deckchair wearing sunglasses.

Alice Tropical Kenya. Straddling the Equator on the Indian Ocean. Enormous open spaces beneath dramatic, ever-changing skies. Unforgettable safaris. And a palm-fringed coast of white coral sand and warm blue waters.

Enter Michel, a French waiter.

Michel Would madame like more wine?
Alice Not half.
Michel Madame?
Alice A full glass.
Michel Very good, madame.
Alice Call me Alice.
Michel Okay, Alice.
Alice And you are?
Michel Michel.
Alice You're French, aren't you, Michel?
Michel Oui, madame.
Alice Alice, please.
Michel Pardonne, Alice.
Alice What's a French waiter doing in Mombasa?
Michel I like to travel. I like to see the beautiful places, and of course, sometimes to meet the very beautiful woman.
Alice We're going to be great friends, Michel.
Michel (*seductively*) Is there anything else you require, Alice?
Alice Such as?

Michel Would you like a top up?

Alice (*pointing to her blouse*) You can get this top up, if you like.

Michel Very good, madame.

Michel leans forward, begins to unbutton her blouse, when Alice loses her nerve.

Alice Stop! Please, go away.

Michel Very good, madame.

Michel exits.

Alice Damn! You bloody fool, Alice. Your own bloody fantasy, and you still haven't got the nerve to go through with it. If you can't get laid in the privacy of your own head, what hope have you got? Now come on, Alice. Relax. This is just pure sex. No strings. No pressure. You don't even need contraception. Maybe just a little more lubrication. (*She takes a big swig of wine*) All right, Michel. This time I'm ready for you. (*Closing her eyes*) Try that seduction line on me again, you smooth-talking Gaul.

Henry (*off-stage*) Bollocks!

A mangled deckchair gets thrown alongside Alice.

Alice On second thoughts, you'd better hide under the bed, Michel. I think I hear an angry husband.

Henry enters. He is wearing a rather unflattering pair of small, tight shorts.

Henry Whoever invented this pile of rotting crap wants stringing up.

Alice Losing your temper isn't going to help.

Henry You want to bet? I mean look at it. All I want to do is sit down. I'm not after mental stimulation. What do I get? A bloody Rubik's deckchair. Over three million combinations. You need a degree in mechanical bloody engineering just to erect the bloody thing.

Alice I'm sure it's easy enough if you keep calm.

Henry Easy enough for you. Yours was already up. First time in two weeks we get any decent weather and I spend all day on this bloody monkey puzzle.

Alice Don't you dare complain about the weather. I told you I wanted to go abroad.

Henry This is abroad.

Alice Wales is not abroad, Henry.

Henry It's not England is it?

Alice It's not Kenya either.

Henry Look, Alice, I won't tell you again. I am not prepared to pay over a thousand pounds for two weeks of flies, famine and disease.

Alice It's not like that.

Henry Course it's like that. Why do you think you have to have three hundred injections before you can even get near the place? Eh? Bloody malaria, typhoid, yellow fever...bloody...whooping cough...God knows what else - I'd look like a sodding pin cushion before I even got on the plane. Bloody Kenya. You're a dreamer, Alice. You really are.

Alice It sounded lovely in the brochure.

Henry Well of course it sounded lovely in the brochure, Alice. They're not going to tell you anything in the brochure, are they? They're not going to say, "Oi, come and blow a thousand quid on a poxy holiday in a disease-ridden cesspit" are they? "Oh, and by the way, just to get you in the holiday mood, stick twenty needles in your arse first." If you want to see a lion you can go to the safari park.

Alice Shut up, I'm trying to enjoy the sun.

Henry Well bully for you. Nice to know one of us has got somewhere to park their bum.

Alice Ask the man. He'll erect it for you.

Henry Huh! No chance.

Alice Why not?

Henry He's Welsh.

Alice What's that got to do with it? He speaks English.

Henry Haven't you got any sense of national pride at all, Alice?

Alice Don't be ridiculous. He's a nice man.

Henry Where's your backbone?

Alice On this deckchair. Where's yours?

Henry Ow! Shit!

Alice What now?

Henry It nearly had my bloody fingers off. This thing's lethal.

Alice Oh, for goodness sake, Henry, just ask the man for another one.

Henry Look at him, he's bloody laughing at me!

Alice He's just smiling, Henry, that's all.

Henry Yes, mate. You'll smile on the other side of your face when I report you to the Health & Safety Executive. They'll have you shut down in seconds, pal. That'll soon wipe your bloody Welsh grin off your mush all right, you

bloody...leek-eating bastard.
Alice Henry! Stop over-reacting. It's just a deckchair.
Henry Yours might be just a deckchair. Mine's a bloody death-trap.
Alice If you're not happy with it, just take it back.
Henry No.
Alice Lie on the floor, then.

Henry tries lying uncomfortably on the floor, head towards the audience, on top of the collapsed deckchair. He keeps wriggling and re-arranging himself.

Alice Can't you keep still?
Henry No.
Alice (*she glances at him from behind her sunglasses, then slowly removes them and gives a long, frowning stare at his shorts*) Henry, for God's sake put your testicle away. It's coming out of the side of your shorts.
Henry If you were any sort of wife you'd rub some Factor 15 on it.
Alice Put it away, Henry. It's horrible.
Henry I like the breeze.
Alice Well don't blame me if that dog comes sniffing round again.
Henry Best offer I've had all fortnight.
Alice It's the only offer you'll get all fortnight, looking like that. Why on earth you didn't let me buy you a new pair of shorts I'll never know.
Henry I feel comfortable in them.
Alice But you're not in them, are you, Henry, that's the problem. You're hanging halfway out of them. It's disgusting. You look like a seagull's laid an egg on you.

Henry wriggles again, re-arranges his shorts, then gets up and has another go at the deckchair.

Henry One pound fifty for this heap of crap.
Alice Talk to the man!
Henry I wouldn't give him the satisfaction.
Alice Then shut up!

Pause.

Henry You ask him.
Alice What?

Henry Well, you're a woman, they expect that sort of thing of women.

Alice gets up, grabs the deckchair and storms off. Henry leaps onto her chair.

Henry Well, I'm sorry, but it's true. Men don't like to admit things like that to men. You know, it's a macho thing. But with women, it's expected. They're supposed to be hopeless at things. This way, nobody gets embarrassed.

We hear Alice, off-stage.

Alice Excuse me, I wonder if you can help me. My husband can't even manage a simple erection.

Lights to black. Lights up to reveal Alice on the settee. She is examining her face through a little hand mirror, applying a little cream from a tub on her lap. Henry is again flicking through channels on the TV.

Henry What the hell's happened to the snooker?
Alice Do I look ten years younger?
Henry Than what? The Shroud of Turin?
Alice At least take a look, Henry.
Henry What am I looking at?
Alice My skin.
Henry *(scrutinising very closely)* What about it?
Alice I've used my new cream. The one with active lipposuction.
Henry Liposomes.
Alice Whatever. What do you think? Has it done anything or not?
Henry Yes, it's knocked about thirty years off your common sense.
Alice What do you mean?
Henry It's a con trick, Alice. That's all it is. A bloody marketing con trick. And you fell for it, hook, line and liposomes.
Alice So what does make you look younger?
Henry Youth.

Alice examines, prods and stretches her skin in the mirror.

Alice Come on, Henry, imagine you're one of those top plastic surgeons in Beverly Hills. What would you recommend for my face?
Henry Amputation.

A Flying Ducks Publication

Alice Forget it.

Henry Usual crap on again tonight.

Alice Did I tell you? Marjorie phoned this afternoon.

Henry I mean, look at him. Stupid sod.

Alice She's pregnant again.

Henry How the hell does he get his own show?

Alice Bit of a shock apparently. She's on the pill, and Derek uses condoms.

Henry I suppose he thinks that's funny.

Alice Not really, he went up the wall.

Henry Who did?

Alice Derek.

Henry Who's Derek?

Alice Derek and Marjorie. She's pregnant.

Henry I know.

Alice How do you know?

Henry I went to the christening, didn't I?

Alice That was the last one. She's pregnant again.

Henry Again? She's got about nineteen kids already.

Alice Three.

Henry Three, nineteen, what's the difference?

Alice Isn't it funny? Marjorie didn't even want children, and she ends up with four.

Henry Hilarious.

Alice And here I am.

Henry Here you are what?

Alice Nothing.

Henry I need a drink.

Henry gets up and moves away. The lights now cut to a moodily spotlit area around the sofa, where Alice stretches out, as if on a pyschiatrist's couch.

Alice We had a good sex life once. No, tell a lie, it was twice. Once on our honeymoon night, and again about three hours later. After that, the novelty seemed to wear off. I'd have given anything to have children, but Henry...

Henry re-enters as the pyschiatrist. He has a clipboard, and sits on a chair beside her.

Psychiatrist What about Henry?

A Flying Ducks Publication

Alice Daren't even bring up the topic.
Psychiatrist Why not?
Alice Just daren't. Not in our house. It's voodoo.
Psychiatrist You mean taboo.
Alice Whatever.
Psychiatrist Have you tried?
Alice What's the use? I know him too well.
Psychiatrist Do you?
Alice Of course I do. I'm married to him, aren't I?
Psychiatrist Do you in some way blame your husband for you not having any children?
Alice No.
Psychiatrist Are you sure?
Alice It takes two not to tango.
Psychiatrist Perhaps you blame yourself.
Alice (*angry*) I don't blame anyone!
Psychiatrist But you regret.
Alice No. Too late to regret.
Psychiatrist So what do you feel?
Alice Nothing. Nothing at all.

The lights fade out. There's a short pause. The phone, situated on a table nearby, rings in the darkness. Alice switches on a lamp by the settee, and checks the time on her watch. She is groggy with sleep, but clearly concerned that it is late, and that Henry doesn't seem to be around.

Alice Henry? Henry? (*She gets up, sits down by the table, and nervously answers the phone*) Hello. Yes. What's happened? Oh, my God!

The lamp fades as Alice replaces the receiver. Suddenly an angle-poise lamp on the table is switched on by Henry, now playing Detective Inspector Blackwell in Alice's ensuing day-dream. The bright light in her face causes Alice to flinch. The lamp alone provides the atmospheric lighting for the scene, which takes the form of a police interrogation. Mr Blackwell is mainly in darkness, except for when he occasionally thrusts his face into the light to emphasize key moments. Alice adopts the demeanour of a hard East End villain.

Blackwell Hello, Alice.
Alice Hello, Mr Blackwell.

Blackwell Detective Inspector Blackwell to you.

Alice I want to see my brief.

Blackwell All in good time, Alice, all in good time. I just want to ask you a few questions.

Alice Like I told your mate, Mr Blackwell, I ain't been nowhere, I ain't done nothing, I ain't seen nothing, I ain't saying nothing.

Blackwell Where's your old man, Alice?

Alice Gawd knows. Down the pub again, if I know him.

Blackwell But you don't know him, do you, Alice - that's the problem.

Alice I don't know what you mean, Mr Blackwell.

Blackwell Stop playing games, Alice. There's a man lying in hospital fighting for his life.

Alice Look, I never touched him.

Blackwell Who said anything about touching him?

Alice What exactly are you accusing me of, Mr Blackwell?

Blackwell Come on, Alice, we both know what we're talking about here, don't we.

Alice Do we?

Blackwell Don't mess me about, Alice. Nagging is a very serious offence.

Alice Look, it ain't down to me.

Blackwell Oh, and I suppose he nagged himself into intensive care, did he?

Alice It was self defence.

Blackwell The judge ain't going to buy that one, Alice. Not this time. We've got a witness.

Alice Oh yeah? Who?

Blackwell Never you mind who.

Alice You're bluffing.

Blackwell Am I?

Alice A witness? That's a sick joke, Mr Blackwell, that is. You see, Henry and me, we never go out together, see. We never have any visitors neither. So where are you going to find a witness, eh?

Blackwell Right...there.

Blackwell points to the goldfish bowl, lit at that moment by a tight spotlight.

Alice You leave my bloody goldfish out of this, copper.

Blackwell He saw everything, Alice. And I reckon he'll testify.

Alice You'd drag an innocent little fish through the courts just to get me?

Blackwell If I had to.

A Flying Ducks Publication

Alice You're wasting your time. Orca's no squealer.

Blackwell Maybe. Maybe not. Don't make me put him on the stand, Alice. I've heard that prosecutor can be a bit of a bastard. Especially if he doesn't like the colour of your skin.

Alice He's just a little goldfish, for God's sake!

Blackwell Then start talking, Alice. And maybe we'll let little Orca swim this one out...whatever that means.

Alice What do you want to know.

The spotlight on the goldfish bowl dims.

Blackwell Why did you go to the hospital today, Alice?

Alice He's my husband, ain't he? I just came to visit.

Blackwell Bullshit. You came to finish him off, didn't you?

Alice I want my brief.

Blackwell Even on his deathbed you couldn't leave him alone, could you, eh?

Alice I want my brief!

Blackwell What was it this time, Alice? Slippers not under the bed? Tubes up his nose not straight enough for you?

Alice Get off my back.

Blackwell What's the matter, Alice? Don't you like the taste of your own poison? (*The phone rings, he answers it*) Blackwell. Right. (*He replaces the receiver*) I'll let you into a little secret, Alice. I was going to let you off with a caution today. Just put the frighteners on a bit. Not any more.

Alice I want to see my lawyer.

Blackwell Well let's hope he's good, Alice. Let's hope he's bloody good. Because you're under arrest for murder.

Alice What?

Blackwell Henry Smith died a few minutes ago.

Alice Oh my God.

Blackwell You're going to get twenty years for this, Alice. Twenty years in solitary.

The lamp fades to darkness, as a distraught Alice weeps into her hands. The phone rings in the darkness. As the lights come up, Alice is asleep awkwardly at the table. She slowly comes round and focuses on the phone, but is obviously very apprehensive about answering, fearing more bad news.

Alice Hello? (*Relief*) Oh, hello, Catherine. Yes, he seemed much better tonight, thank you, yes. They reckon he could be out by Friday. I've got a special diet for him. And he's got some little red tablets to take - that's for his blood pressure. Anyway, the consultant says the main thing is to avoid stress.

The lights instantly cut to show Henry, sitting at a desk, as the stressed business executive. Powerful, fast-talking and uncompromisingly bad-tempered, he is screaming down the phone.

Executive Look, I will not have you messing up my Overseas operation with your bloody cavalier attitude, Clive, am I making myself clear? Good! Now sort yourself out, stop making up company policy on the fly - and get me some results by Friday or it's goodnight Vienna! (*He slams down the phone and reaches for the intercom*) Carol! Now!

Carol, the beleaguered secretary, enters, armed with a note-pad and pencil.

Carol Yes, sir?
Executive Get me Norman Hardy on the phone - right away.
Carol I'm afraid Norman's not in today.
Executive He's what?
Carol He's not in today, sir.
Executive Do we know why?
Carol I think he's ill.
Executive You think he's ill.
Carol Yes, sir.
Executive So who's out there?
Carol I don't know, sir.
Executive Do I pay you not to know, Carol?
Carol I don't know, sir.
Executive Get hold of Eric Johnson, tell him I want someone out there covering East Region - now!
Carol Yes, sir.
Executive Not yet! Diary.
Carol Oh, right. You've got a nine-thirty with John Deeley of Sutherlands. A one o'clock with Mr Wainwright at his club...
Executive Oh, bugger! Carry on.
Carol A two-fifteen with Mike Drummond...
Executive Shit! Shit! Shit! Bloody Unions! Shit and bugger! Bugger and shit!

Yes, yes.

Carol A three-thirty with marketing, and a four-fifteen at Chepstow...no, sorry, that's just your...(*she fumbles with a betting slip*)

Executive All right, listen up. Cancel the Chairman. Put the unions back to three o'clock. Tell them I've only got half an hour. Plane to catch. Whatever you like. Ditch marketing. Call a crisis meeting with John Tobey. One o'clock. My office. Order some sandwiches. Ham, brown bread, salad, no onion. Coffee. De-caffeinated. Phone my wife, tell her I'll be late. Send some flowers. Roses. Red not pink. Just one. No calls. Read that back.

Carol (*scribbling furiously into her shorthand note-pad*) Erm..."Shit and bugger, bugger and shit...

Executive Never mind, get on with it, and get out.

Carol Oh, what do I tell the Chairman?

Executive (*tetchily*) Tell him I've got a business to run. I'm sure he'll understand. Move it.

Carol (*going to exit*) Yes, sir.

Executive Oh, and Carol...(*handing her a huge wad of papers*)...get this typed up first.

Carol is now Henry's female boss.

Female Boss I beg your pardon!

Henry Oh, I'm sorry, I er...I was miles away.

Female Boss What are you doing at my desk?

Henry Nothing, I was just...looking...for something. Some papers. (*Taking the papers back from her*) Found them.

Female Boss (*snatching the papers back again*) You've got no right to be looking at this stuff.

Henry No, I'm sorry, I made a mistake.

Female Boss You certainly have, Henry. This is the third time I've had to talk to you about your...peculiar behaviour. Now, I'll ask you just once more. What were you doing in my office?

A pause, and Henry adopts a self-assured smile, and becomes Henry Bond, secret agent.

Bond And what if I refuse to talk?

The female boss becomes a Russian agent, who takes out a gun from her handbag.

Russian Agent Well, maybe this will help loosen your tongue.
Bond Well, well. Katrina Dobrinski. Showing your true colours at last.
Russian Agent Over by the wall, Mr...
Bond Bond. Henry Bond.
Russian Agent Hands.

He puts his hands in the air. She starts frisking him.

Bond If you're looking for a loaded weapon, you're searching too high.
Russian Agent The microfilm, please, Mr Bond.
Bond Certainly.

He grabs a biro from his coat pocket, clicks the button, throws it to the ground and prepares himself for an explosion. Nothing happens.

Russian Agent You've dropped your pen, Mr Bond.
Bond Bloody gadgets.
Russian Agent The microfilm.
Bond I'm afraid I haven't got it.
Russian Agent In that case, I'm going to have to shoot you.
Bond Of course. But before you do, how about raw sex on a white fur rug?
Russian Agent (*dropping the gun*) Oh, Henry!

Henry grabs her, and rolls onto the settee. But instantly she reverts back to the female boss, and stands, leaving him sprawled out.

Female Boss What the bloody hell do you think you're doing?
Henry Shit!

Lights to black. Moody lighting reveals, once again, the psychiatrist's office, complete with slow-ticking clock. This time, however, it is Henry on the couch, with the studious, bespectacled female psychiatrist sat beside him.

Psychiatrist And how long have you been out of work now, Mr Smith?
Henry (*a deep sigh*) Since...erm...since Thursday afternoon.
Psychiatrist And what made you feel you wanted to see a psychiatrist, rather than a doctor?
Henry I saw the doctor.
Psychiatrist And what did he say?

Henry He gave me some antibiotics.

Psychiatrist I see. So, why are you here?

Henry I'm going mad.

Psychiatrist I doubt that, Mr Smith.

Henry Why?

Psychiatrist Because you're aware of it. People who are genuinely mad are not usually aware that they're mad. It's only sane people that think they're mad.

Henry So, as long as I keep thinking I'm mad, I'm probably sane?

Psychiatrist Yes, basically. The time to worry is when you think you're sane, and other people think you're mad.

Henry Do you think I'm mad?

Psychiatrist It's a little early for a professional diagnosis.

Henry I've been trying to do things, you know, around the house, little things, just to stop me from going mad, but...

Psychiatrist But what?

Henry Well, I just seem to be driving my wife mad.

Psychiatrist What does your wife do?

Henry She's a housewife.

Psychiatrist Full-time?

Henry Overtime.

Psychiatrist Well, perhaps you should try a few outdoor activities instead. Somewhere the two of you wouldn't clash.

Henry I tried a spot of gardening yesterday.

Psychiatrist Gardening. Excellent. Very therapeutic.

Henry Not the way I do it. I set fire to the lawn.

Psychiatrist (*closing her eyes in disbelief*) How did you set fire to the lawn, Mr Smith?

Henry Not my fault. The lawnmower had a bit of a leak in the petrol tank. I'd done the whole lot. Looked very nice. All stripey. Just stood back to admire my work, lit a cigarette. Three fire engines it took. Next door neighbour's fence went up as well. And his tree. And his cat. He was up the tree. Petrol tank exploded. Straight through the kitchen window. Set fire to the curtains. Spoilt the haddock. New trousers they were.

Psychiatrist What did your wife say?

Henry She said I was mad. Wearing new trousers to do the lawn. Anyway, I'm not going to sit around talking about Alice. It's a waste of a good fantasy. Take your clothes off.

Psychiatrist Sorry, Mr Smith, I'm not one of your fantasy creations.

Henry Aren't you?

A Flying Ducks Publication

Psychiatrist You tell me.

Henry I don't know. It's getting harder to work out which bits are real and which bits are just in my head.

Psychiatrist Just because something only happens in your head, it doesn't mean it isn't real.

Henry All right, so it's real. But it's not the truth.

Psychiatrist So what is the truth, Henry? What are you really doing, right now?

Henry I'm dozing, probably. On this settee. Half asleep, half awake.

Psychiatrist And Alice. What's she doing?

Henry The housework. Always the housework. I remember once I was lying on this settee, in my pyjamas, and this nubile, naked woman was licking her way down my torso, inch by inch. That's fairly normal for a Sunday afternoon. Anyway, she got about halfway down and suddenly I felt the fly of my pyjama trousers burst open, and there was this most glorious, wet, warm sucking sensation. It felt so extraordinary, so real, I just had to open my eyes. I looked down. Couldn't believe what I saw. It was Alice.

Psychiatrist Alice?

Henry Yes. She'd borrowed next-door's Vax to clean the upholstery on the settee. The doorbell had rung. She'd dropped everything to dash off and answer it and, well, you can guess the rest.

Psychiatrist That's horrible.

Henry Yes. The vicar didn't know which way to turn. Still, you've got to give those Vaxes their due - it came up a treat. I offered to get Alice one for Christmas, but she didn't want to know. (*Peering over her clipboard*) You do think I'm mad, don't you.

Psychiatrist No.

Henry What's this then, eh? First thing you've written. Fruitcake.

Psychiatrist That's my shopping list, Mr Smith.

Henry And what's that say, right underneath?

Psychiatrist (*reluctantly*) Bananas.

Henry And nuts! You've written nuts!

Psychiatrist Mr Smith, I do not think you're mad. Just a bit...

Henry A bit what? Go on, say it!

Psychiatrist A bit...boring. Okay? You were boring me to death, so I started writing my shopping list.

Henry Are you sure you can't take your clothes off?

Psychiatrist I think you need to rest, Henry.

Henry Rest? I'm probably asleep!

Psychiatrist Rest your mind. Switch off for a while. You've got a big day tomorrow.

Henry Have I?

Psychiatrist Very big. Something very important's going to happen tomorrow. Anyway, you've got to visit the Queen.

Henry The Queen? What's the Queen got to do with it?

Psychiatrist (*stroking his brow gently*) Shhh. Close your eyes.

Henry (*mumbling, half asleep*) I'm not seeing the Queen. What's all this about the Queen?

Psychiatrist Shhh. Get some rest.

She quietly fades away into the shadows, leaving Henry dozing on the settee, still mumbling indiscernibly about the Queen, as the end of the National Anthem fades up and the lights fade down to just the flicker of the television on his face. It ends, and gives way to the high-pitched tone of the television announcing the end of the day's broadcasting. This eventually rouses Henry, who wakes feeling ghastly and with a stiff neck. He grumpily gets up, switches off the television, and disappears to bed. Lights up to reveal Alice polishing. She squirts polish onto Orca's goldfish bowl.

Alice There's, that's better, isn't it, Orca. I've re-arranged the dirt. That'll keep you amused for another three or four weeks. Poor little thing. (*She sighs a deep, tired sigh, and sinks down into the settee. The lights close down to a glow around the settee. She closes her eyes, and stretches out her arm holding the furniture polish*) Michel, rub this hot oil into my breasts, there's a good chap. But start with the shoulders. I don't want you to think I'm forward.

Henry steps out of the darkness and puts his hand on her shoulder. She jumps.

Alice Arrgh! Oh God, it's you.

Henry Who did you think it was?

Alice You scared me.

Henry You scared *me*. I thought you'd had a funny turn.

Alice Why?

Henry Sitting there with that inane grin on your face. I thought you'd died.

Alice No. I just started living for a moment.

Henry I want you to massage me.

Alice Do what?

Henry With this Deep Heat stuff. Just massage it in my neck.

Alice What's the matter with your neck?

A Flying Ducks Publication

Henry Don't know. I must have slept funny.
Alice You always sleep funny.
Henry I must have slept normally for one night, then. Just rub it in.
Alice It stinks.
Henry Come on. I'm in agony.
Alice (*reluctantly rubbing in the lotion*) It serves you right. A man of your age throwing melons about. You've probably pulled something.
Henry It's not easy to pull anything at my age. (*He looks over at the goldfish bowl*) Orca? (*He gets up and moves over to the bowl*)
Alice What's the matter?
Henry He's dead.
Alice What? (*Alice joins Henry at the bowl*) Oh, no! Do something, Henry!
Henry Like what?
Alice I don't know. First aid. Give him artificial restoration or something.
Henry He's not drowned, Alice - he's a bloody fish.
Alice He was all right a minute ago. I dusted his bowl.
Henry Well, he's not all right now.
Alice Oh, Henry!
Henry That's your lot, is it, Orca? Given up on us, have you?
Alice We finally bored you to death.
Henry Oh, well. I don't suppose he had anything exciting planned for tomorrow.

They crouch down, staring into the goldfish bowl, as if it were a crystal ball. The lights fade, and the bowl, which is under-lit from its stand, starts to glow surreally. There's the sound of a noisy fairground, enhanced by swirling lighting effects, such as a mirrorball. Alice momentarily becomes a fairground lady, before she and Henry are both transformed into their young selves.

Fairground Lady Three hoops for a pound. Three hoops for a pound. Come on, son, how about trying to win a prize for the young lady? Three goes for just a pound.
Young Henry But the prizes are only worth ten bob.
Fairground Lady That's hardly the spirit, is it? Come on, show us what you're made of.
Young Henry No, thanks.
Young Alice Oh, go on, Henry, you haven't had a go on anything yet.
Young Henry Oh, all right. Here you go.

A Flying Ducks Publication

Henry hands over a coin, picks up three hoops, and tosses the first.   There's momentary excitement, and disappointment.

Young Alice Try one of the nearer ones.
Young Henry It's a con. They won't go over.

He tosses the second.

Young Alice Oh! Nearly!
Young Henry No chance. Last one.

Alice jumps up in youthful excitement. Even Henry can't resist joining in.

Young Alice Yes!
Young Henry Hey, missus! Over here! Number ten!
Young Alice What have we got?
Young Henry Oh, no! Not a bloody goldfish!
Young Alice That one. I want that one. (*She gives Henry a big kiss on the cheek*) My hero!
Young Henry Alice...
Young Alice What?
Young Henry Perhaps this isn't the right time.
Young Alice What? (*Shouting to the fairground lady*) No, that one, on the end.
Young Henry I was wondering if you fancied marrying me, at all, sometime, perhaps. Or perhaps not.

Alice turns, open-mouthed, to Henry, and stares.

Young Henry Shut your mouth. You look like a goldfish.

Alice, thrilled, flings her arms around Henry, and starts kissing him. It turns into a passionate embrace. The lighting and fairground effects fade away.

Alice Henry...
Henry Alice...
Alice Henry, what are we doing?
Henry (*in a French accent*) Relax, Mrs Robinson. Let me rub in the oil.
Alice Michel? Michel, is that you?
Henry Non, madame, it's me, Henri the waiter.

Alice Oh, Michel, I've waited so long.
Henry You need a little more on your breasts.
Alice Of course. *(She suddenly pushes Henry away)* Who's Mrs Robinson?
Henry Who's Michel?
Alice How do you know about Michel?
Henry You called me Michel.
Alice Did I?
Henry Yes.
Alice Well, you were talking in a French accent. You said you were a waiter.
Henry So that makes me Michel, does it?
Alice Don't avoid the question.
Henry What question?
Alice Who's Mrs Robinson?
Henry Nobody. Just a friend of Henri.
Alice Who's Henri?
Henry A French waiter. I made him up. It's a daydream, that's all.
Alice You daydream about French waiters?
Henry Look, forget it. I don't want to talk about it.
Alice So do I.
Henry What?
Alice Michel. I met him in Kenya.
Henry Kenya?
Alice Well, it's cheaper than the real thing. And you don't need the injections.
Henry I'm confused.
Alice Look, I've never been to bed with him, Henry, I promise, we're just good friends.
Henry I've read about them, but I never thought they really existed.
Alice What, French waiters?
Henry No. Two-way dreams.
Alice What?
Henry It's where one person dreams about something, and the other person - the one they're dreaming about - is also dreaming the same dream, but from their point of view.
Alice Is this another one of your interesting facts, Henry?
Henry Yes.
Alice It's very interesting.
Henry It's bloody fascinating, that's what it is.
Alice Do you daydream a lot?
Henry Sometimes.

Alice What about?

Henry Everything. Life. Death.

Alice Other women?

Henry Yes, sometimes, other women. (*As if realizing for the first time*) It's a funny thing though, Alice - every time I dream about other women, they always look like you.

Alice That's the niftiest bit of footwork I've seen in a long time, Henry.

Henry No, it's true.

They hug.

Alice Look, Henry, at the risk of sounding a little forward, I do find you outrageously attractive, and I'd very much like you to pluck me up in your strong arms, tear the clothes from my thrashing limbs, toss me like a rag doll onto the sofa, and roger me senseless.

Henry (*amazed*) What made you say that?

Alice Oh, just a daydream I once had. I was at a party, and I met a man...

Henry This is weird. Have you ever had a daydream about American Football?

Alice Don't tell me - you were the big guy who throws the ball.

Henry The quarterback.

Alice That's right.

Henry I won the game in the last minute.

Alice I was more interested in what happened after the game.

Henry You know about that?

Alice I was that cheerleader.

Henry This...is really weird. Mrs Smith, there's a lot more to you than meets the eye.

Alice Mr Smith, how would you like to rub hot oil into my breasts?

Henry Would you settle for Deep Heat?

Alice The deeper the better.

Henry starts to unbutton Alice's blouse and, at a critical moment, stops and turns to the audience.

Henry You find your own bloody fantasy!

Lights to black. Curtain.

A Flying Ducks Publication